HIS GOOD PLEASURE

ACCESSING THE KINGDOM YOU HAVE BEEN GIVEN!

JACOB BISWELL

Jacob Biswell
ISBN-13: 978-0692748220
ISBN-10: 0692748229

To contact the author
Jacob Biswell
www.jacobbiswell.com
jacobbiswell@yahoo.com
3205 Lakeview St. Bryan, TX 77801

DEDICATION

My wife – Anna Katheryn. Your tireless
support and help in my many "Projects"
is priceless. Your love, your tenacity,
your faith – it is these things that
inspire me to keep going!

I love you!

Acknowledgements

Kim Hembry – Your ability to take
words and help form art is uncanny!
Thank you!

Birdella Tucker – Releasing me at such
a young age to learn truth proved to
worth it! Thank you!

Table of Contents

Introduction

Key 1 – It's His Will

Key 2 – Understanding the Covenant

Key 3 - You're Worthy to Receive

Key 4 – The Power of Testimony

Key 5 – Hindrances to Breakthrough

Key 6 – Understanding Your Authority

Key 7 – Dealing with the Spirit

Key 8 – Overcoming the Past

Key 9 – Tenacity

Key 10 – Obedience

Final Key

Keys to Victory

"Fear not, little flock; for it is your Father's good pleasure to give you the Kingdom..."

LUKE 12:32

INTRODUCTION

God gets pleasure out of giving me the Kingdom – What a concept. The happiest the Father can be is to give you the Kingdom. What is the Kingdom? It's arms growing back. It's financial miracles. It's supernatural encounters. It's Him. The Bible says, "Seek first the Kingdom, and then everything else comes to you." (Matthew 6:33)

If it's the Father's good pleasure to give you the Kingdom, when you seek it, it's easy to find.

The Kingdom isn't hidden somewhere where we have to go on some long journey. There are people on the Earth who have to travel long distances to find their god. But it has become clear in my journey that my God came a long distance to find me. The Bible says He left his throne to come to Earth for you and me (Phil. 2:7-8). So if He took that long journey for you and me, when we seek His Kingdom, He's going to give it in full measure.

When the Kingdom comes upon you, it transforms your life. When the Kingdom manifests in front of you, you can't help but be transformed. In His Kingdom is everything we have need of. It's my desire for you to access that Kingdom and in doing so, access all He paid for. My prayer is that you will receive keys to accessing the Kingdom you have been given… because it really is *His Good Pleasure!*

Jacob Biswell

-KEY 1-

IT'S HIS WILL

I'll never forget her face when God set her free of unbearable back pain that had plagued her for over 15 years. She kept saying, "Well, I've prayed before, but I just don't know if it's God's will to heal me." I had to stop her – I said, "You've got to believe it is his will." She looked at me as though I had offended her – she got angry. She kind of snarled, "Well fine then, I believe it is His will." Then God healed her! It is always God's will to heal!

The Father's will for your life is to give you the Kingdom. Imagine with me coming to your best friend and finding out that they had the ability to heal your body. But before you let them do anything, you say, "Now, you only have to do this if it's your will." Can you imagine the shock on their face? "What do you mean? Of course it's my will, you're my best friend!"

So it is with the Father. We often stop the work of His hand because we come with this idea, that it may not be His will to heal us. The church has been the biggest perpetuator of the lie that it may not be God's will to heal, bless, provide, etc. You name it and the church has put limitations on when, how, why and even where God will move on your behalf.

I remember speaking with another woman one time in a grocery store. She was visibly in pain and I approached her to ask her if I could pray for her. Her response floored me. She said, "No, you may not. If God was going to heal me, he certainly wouldn't do it here, it would have to be *my* pastor at the altar of *my* church." I tried to reason with her, but she would not have it. She went on her way, still in pain because "God couldn't move in a grocery store." It had more to do with her own unbelief that it was actually God's will to heal her, than it had to do with where we were.

Most churches teach that it is not always the will of God to heal you; it is not likely that you will trust God for your healing if you have not heard this truth taught. If you have not been exposed to Truth, it is pretty hard to believe Truth. Faith comes and is developed through hearing and hearing the Word of God (Romans 10:17).

If you need a healing, you need to get into the Word of God - Ignorance of the Word of God and ignorance of the Covenant that He has made with you, will prevent you from receiving your healing.

In the book of Matthew, a leper approaches Jesus and says, "If you are willing, I know I will be made whole..." I can just imagine the twinkle in His eye as Jesus responds, "I am willing, be made whole..." (Matthew 8)

It is His will and He is willing!

-KEY 2-

UNDERSTAND THE COVENANT

The concept of **Covenant** is important in receiving the Kingdom you have been given, especially in the realm of healing.

Exodus 15:26 states, "If you will diligently listen and pay attention to the voice of the Lord your God, and do what is right in His sight, and listen to His commandments, and keep [foremost in your thoughts and actively obey] all His precepts and statutes, then I will not put on you any of the diseases which I have put on the Egyptians; for I am the Lord who heals you." (AMP)

What a promise! Jesus established the New Covenant

the night before his crucifixion. Jesus said to his disciples at the Last Supper, "this is my blood of the New Covenant, which is shed for many for the remission of sins" [Matthew 26:26-28, Mark 20:22-24, Luke 22:18-20, and 1 Corinthians 11:23-26].

Jesus is the mediator of a better Covenant, which was established upon better promises. IF forgiveness of sins, physical healing, deliverance, favor, provisional care, fruitfulness, and long life were spiritual blessings of the Old Covenant; how much more are they in the New Covenant which has the Holy Spirit as the Guarantor of this better Covenant? (Eph. 1:14)

He wants to transform your life. See, sickness died at the cross. The Bible says He was bruised and crushed, and the chastisement of our peace was upon Him. By His stripes we were healed. Your healing already happened at the cross. It's already finished. There is nothing you can do to earn your healing. All you have to do is agree.

When you buy a house, you have to sign your name quite a few times. When you buy a car, especially when you finance it, you've got to sign your name quite a few times. Well, when Jesus died, He created a new Covenant, and all you have to do is sign your life away. All you have to do is say, "I agree to the terms of this Covenant." In exchange for your life, you get joy. You get healing. You get provision. You get reconciliation. You get your family restored. You get everything in the Covenant. All He asks for is your life.

You know, that's a pretty uneven exchange. We get all of Him, and He gets us. I've thought sometimes, "Lord, I don't think you really know what you're doing here. I get your Kingdom, and you get me? That seems pretty unfair, God." And He said, "I love you that much that I'll take you. But remember, I created you. I created your personality. I love to work with you."

You've got to understand that it's a Covenant written in blood, a Covenant that was finished at the cross. All you've got to do is sign your name to it. You say, "Jesus, You get all of me, and I get all of you."

-Key 3-

You're Worthy to Receive

One of the things religion has done is put so much emphasis on our performance that most of us, quite frankly, doubt our right standing with God. What religion has in fact done, is cast doubt and unbelief on the work that Jesus did for us on the Cross. God's Word tells us that in Christ, we are not under any condemnation, but that our sins are totally forgiven! The scriptural fact is that we are created in Christ's righteousness and true holiness!

"...and put on the new self [the regenerated and renewed nature], created in God's image, [godlike] in the righteousness and holiness of the truth [living in a way that expresses to God your gratitude for your salvation]..." (Ephesians 3:24 AMP)

I like how Joseph Prince shared that He used to preach the things which will hinder a healing, until the Holy Spirit spoke to him and told him to stop disqualifying His people. Once he began to preach that we are worthy to receive our healing because of what Jesus has done for us, healings broke out everywhere in His church! This embraces the fact that what Jesus did determines our relationship with God and not our performance. If we continue to give in to sin and seek after the flesh, we will die spiritually (Romans 8:13), but for those of us who are seeking after the things of God in our lives (those of us walking after the Spirit, or seeking after the Spirit of God in our lives), we are worthy to receive all the promises of God because of the cleansing work of Christ in our lives. There is no condemnation in us!

"There is therefore now no condemnation to them which are in Christ Jesus, who walk not after the flesh, but after the Spirit." (Romans 8:1 KJV)

One of the biggest hindrances to receiving our

healing or any other promise of the Covenant we have with God, is whether or not we see ourselves as worthy to receive the promises of God. If we have been cleansed by the Blood of Christ, and yet still see ourselves as unworthy, we are then in unbelief concerning the cleansing work of Christ. He has paid for the total forgiveness of all our sins! This kind of unbelief kills your faith and ability to believe God for the other promises of the Covenant we share with Him. You won't have faith to believe God for a healing, if you don't feel worthy to receive the promise of healing that was included in the New Covenant. The promise of forgiveness of sins is the foundation we have to believe for all the other benefits of the New Covenant!

Our sufficiency (or our worthiness to receive) is ONLY because of Christ's work for us, and nothing that we have done can make us worthy for all the promises of God:

"Not that we are sufficient of ourselves to think anything as of ourselves; but our sufficiency [worthiness] is of God." (2 Corinthians 3:5 KJV)

The letter of the law disqualifies us, but the Spirit

gives us life in Christ! The Ten Commandments were said to be the ministry of condemnation and death:

"Who also hath made us able ministers of the New Covenant; not of the letter, but of the spirit: for the letter killeth, but the spirit giveth life. But if the ministration of death, written and engraven in stones, was glorious, so that the children of Israel could not steadfastly behold the face of Moses for the glory of his countenance; which glory was to be done away: How shall not the ministration of the spirit be rather glorious? For if the ministration of condemnation be glory, much more doth the ministration of righteousness exceed in glory." (2 Corinthians 3:6-9 KJV)

We are justified through faith in the work of Christ, not by the works (or obedience to) the law. Our performance gets us nowhere in qualifying us to receive the promises of God!

"Knowing that a man is not justified by the works of the law, but by the faith of Jesus Christ, even we have believed in Jesus Christ, that we might be justified by the faith of Christ, and not by the works of the law: for by the works of the law shall no flesh be justified." (Galatians 2:16 KJV)

Religion and the law disqualifies those who Christ has qualified. If you want faith to receive the promises of the New Covenant, such as healing, then you're going to have to stop looking to your performance to make you worthy, and start looking to the finished work of the Cross. What happens when we hear the message of Christ's atoning work? Faith arises in our soul, because we begin to realize that He paid the price and made us worthy to receive all the good things that God has for us!

"So then faith cometh by hearing, and hearing by the word of God." (Romans 10:17 KJV)

And if you look at the context, it is NOT talking about the Bible in general, but rather specifically the gospel and finished work of Christ. Go read for yourself verses 3 through 16 and you'll realize that verse 17 has everything to do with the New Covenant and righteousness by faith in the Cross!

-KEY 4-

THE POWER OF
THE TESTIMONY

'They overcame him by the blood of the Lamb and by the word of their testimony; they did not love their lives so much as to shrink from death."
Revelation 12:11

You know, it doesn't matter who you are. It doesn't matter where you've been. There is nothing that intimidates Him. Your sickness isn't too big for Him. Your situation isn't too big for Him. The Bible says in Revelation 19:10 that the spirit of prophecy is the testimony of Jesus. So I'm going to share a couple of testimonies to build your faith.

Now, for some of you, you may think to yourself,

"How is that possible?" I serve a God of the impossible. I serve a God who defies human logic. I serve a God who walked on water. He defies gravity. He defies human intellect.

So I ask one thing from you. Just be open to receive from Him. In 2004, I was on a mission trip to Mexico, and I was believing for God to do something great. Well, six days into the trip, I hadn't even seen a headache healed. We took the bus on a four drive out to a little village. We got there, and we gave the Gospel message. I said, "Lord, I need to see you move. I want to see your Kingdom come." About that time, little Laura walked around the corner.

Laura was a beautiful little girl, about nine or ten years old. She had something that was very noticeable. She was missing half of her left arm. I said, "Lord, that's the one! She needs her arm back!"

I had never prayed for an arm to come back. I'd never seen an arm come back. But I knew that God was going to do it. I went up to Laura, and in my broken Spanish, I said something like, "¿Su queres tu brazo?" I think that's about right. "Do you want your arm?"

I'll never forget her face. I didn't know what else to say at that point. So whether she wanted it or not, I grabbed what was left, that little stump. I said, "Arm, grow in Jesus' name."

Well, I did not know that it was going to grow. Right there before my eyes, a bone popped out, and I was shocked. In about 45 seconds to about a minute-and-a-half – it seemed like it was slow motion for me – I watched as that bone grew and a skeleton formed. I watched as the muscle began to shape around that bone. I watched as the skin grew out across that muscle. Then I watched as her fingernails grew out.

In Psalm 37, it says, "God delights in the details of your life." So not only did God give her an arm back, He grew her fingernails out to the same length as the other hand and gave her a whole manicure and painted her fingernails for her. They were the same hot pink on the left hand that were on the right hand because God delighted in the details of her life. It is His good pleasure to give you the Kingdom. It is His good pleasure to manifest Himself.

In 2009 - I'm in a little mountain church ministering

and this man comes up. He looked perfectly normal to me. He says, "I want my eye back." I said, "You have an eye." He said, "No, that's a glass eye." I said, "Well, they did a good job," because I could not tell. I said, "Well, God can do it. I know He can." Listen, even being a man of faith, God still stretches me sometimes. So I put my hand on that eye, and I didn't know if God was going to pop it out or what was going to happen. So I said, "In the name of Jesus, eye return to this socket," and that glass eye began to spin. When it stopped spinning, I heard this, "I can see!" God recreated that eye.

Another one of my favorite testimonies happened the same night as the new eye. A woman who was in a wheelchair kept moaning through most of my message. It honestly began to bother me. So in the middle of my message, I went over and asked her what was causing her so much pain. She looked up at me, no hope in her eyes and said, "I fell and broke my hip. I don't have insurance and they won't allow me to have surgery. I'm in excruciating pain and I don't know what to do." The Lord spoke to me and said, "Tell her to stand up!" I said to the woman, "Stand up." Horrified, she muttered, "I can't! My hip is in pieces, I will fall over." The Lord again impressed me to tell her to stand up, so I said it again, "Stand up, I will make sure you don't fall. The Lord is going to heal you, but you have to stand up." She grimaced, but with every ounce of strength, she wobbled forward out of the wheelchair and stood up with the assistance of a few strong men. The Lord then spoke to me, "grab her hip and feel the bone moving around." I quickly obeyed. I could feel the bone moving around but as I moved it around it began to take shape. Within a few seconds, the bone was completely back in place and she was no longer in pain. I was stunned, not because I didn't think he could do, but because I got to feel the bone be put back in place. She began to weep, then she began to laugh, then she began to jump, then she began to run. The very woman who had become a distraction because of her pain was now running down the aisles, COMPLETELY HEALED!

God delights in the details of your life. Whatever it is that you are believing God for, whatever it is that you need – take these testimonies as a prophetic word over your life that if He did it for them, He will do it for you!

-Key 5-

Hindrances to Breakthrough

Hindrance One: Traditionalism!

"Jesus left there and came to His hometown [Nazareth]; and His disciples followed Him. When the Sabbath came, He began to teach in the synagogue; and many who listened to Him were astonished, saying, "Where did this man get these things [this knowledge and spiritual insight]? What is this wisdom [this confident understanding of the Scripture] that has been given to Him, and such miracles as these performed by His hands?" (Mk.6:1-2)

There are a lot of people who look at their tradition and say, "that's not how my church does it" or "that's not how I was taught."

As long as you treat your tradition as more sacred than the Word of God, you will stop the flow of God on your behalf. Any kind of tradition that has its origins in a "works-mentality" can be a hindrance to receiving whatever it is that God has for you – this includes the law of the Old Covenant. Many people will reject anything that is contrary to the teachings of their denomination. I like to say, "God likes barbeque and He has no issue roasting your religious cow!"

Traditions of men will shut down the healing and supernatural power of God in His church. We find that when Jesus entered Nazareth, he was unable to do many miracles. Tradition held them in their unbelief. In contrast, when Jesus entered Capernaum, they not being hindered by tradition openly received the miracles of God.

Hindrance Two: Sin
(Mk.6:12; 11:25; Pr.3:7-8)

It is important to turn your back on sin - an unrepentant heart can hinder healing. Are you clean before the Lord? Sometimes people have a known sin in their lives that they refuse to deal with. We stand in the righteousness of Jesus - but that does not give us the license to sin. We must flee youthful lusts. If we are knowingly and willfully walking in disobedience, healing can be delayed or withheld all together. When Jesus healed the blind man He told him, "Go and sin no more lest a worse thing come upon you" (John 5:14). Sin hinders healing and can cause an open door for the devil to attack you with sickness.

In my experience, the most common sin in the believer's life is unforgiveness. If you are not in right standing with your brothers, it hinders the flow of the power of God. Jesus said that if you expect Him to forgive you, you must forgive others. Unity in the body of Christ is important in order for His supernatural power to flow.

Therefore, live righteously by walking in the spirit

and not in the flesh (Romans 8:1-11).

The Bible says in Psalm 84:11 (KJV), "No good thing will He withhold from those who walk uprightly."

You want to know how to walk uprightly? Seek the Kingdom. That's the easiest way to stay out of sin. Seek the Kingdom because when you're seeking the Kingdom, you're seeking Him. When your focus is on Him, you can't sin because you won't be distracted by the things that cause you to sin. It is possible to live a life where sin has no hold on you by seeking the Kingdom.

Hindrance Three: Lack of Faith or Unbelief!
(Mk.6:5-6; 9:23; Mt.14:31; 21:21)

Lack of faith is one of the biggest hindrances to divine healing. Faith is a major requirement to releasing the power of God on your behalf. Unbelief resists the healing power of God for your life. Many Christians are unbelieving believers. Even the disciples could not see miracles because of their lack of faith and Jesus even rebuked them for it.

Perhaps you basically believe the promises of God, but you have entertained the many doubts that are thrown into your mind either by society, by satan, or from other sources. If you don't stay diligently grounded in the Word, doubt will begin to enter in.

It's very important that you're not wavering (James.1:6-8) in faith, but are "fully persuaded" (Rm.4). Some speak words of faith, but their actions contradict their words (James 2). Some speak words of faith when they are around other faith walking people, but take them out of that environment and they lose all talk of faith. Their thoughts are no different. One moment they believe, the next they are agreeing with thoughts of fear and unbelief. These people are double minded. Scripture makes it clear that they will not receive anything from God.

Hindrance Four: Fear!

(Mt.6)

Worry and fear is the opposite of faith - it's faith in reverse - believing the wrong things. Worry and fear will produce ulcers and other health problems - it is working against you. There is no fear in faith - perfect love will cast out all fear - and faith works by love. You cannot be in faith and fear at the same time. So fear is another manifestation of unbelief.

Hindrance Five: Negative Confessions!
(Pr.6; 18; Jas.3; Is.55:11)

The words of your mouth reveal your faith - If you are walking in faith, it'll show. It is critically important that we say about ourselves what God's Word says about us - If God says we are healed, it is okay for us to say we are healed, regardless of how we feel. It's imperative that we consistently confess the Word - our words give us direction and He watches over His Word to perform it on our behalf. We must continually speak His Word over our situations.

Ultimately, no matter the hindrance, it pales in comparison to the authority Jesus has placed on the inside of you. In the next chapter, we discuss your authority and how to overcome these hindrances.

-Key 6-

Understanding Your Authority

Our authority is based on Jesus' victory. At the cross, Jesus as a man defeated satan and all demonic principalities and made a public spectacle of them before the audience of heaven, hell and earth. This victory IS finished!

When He had disarmed the rulers and authorities [those supernatural forces of evil operating against us], He made a public example of them [exhibiting them as captives in His triumphal procession], having triumphed over them through the cross. (Col. 2:15, AMP)

Our spiritual authority is based on our union with Jesus (John 15). The power and benefits Jesus received as a man raised from the dead are given to us. God gave Jesus to the church as our head and made us His body to express his power to the earth.

We have been raised to sit with Jesus in heavenly places and are given access to God's throne. When we pray, we release the authority AND power based on our union with Christ. We must know who we are in Christ and the authority we possess in Jesus. We must take our place of authority in Christ as those seated in heavenly places with Jesus. (Eph. 2:6)

Authority is a delegated power. An example that is commonly used is that of a police officer who stops a car by the authority of the government, not by his own physical power.

As Jesus' body, we are called to enforce His authority on the earth. As we walk in our identity rooted in him, then those things that would try and hinder us are dethroned from our thinking and we take on the Mind of Christ. Our authority is based on what Jesus accomplished, not on anything less.

If you search the entire New Covenant, you will find

that there is very little said about praying for the sick. As a matter of fact, I am only aware of one scripture that even uses the words praying for the sick and that is James 5:15. All of the other scriptures and examples we find in Jesus' ministry and that of the early church has to do more with using authority and speaking commands to be healed. Jesus never prayed to the Father asking Him to heal somebody, He spoke to the person and said something like, "Rise up and walk!" The early church did the same thing, except they added the name of Jesus. Peter didn't pray for the lame man to be healed, he spoke to the man saying, "In the name of Jesus Christ of Nazareth rise up and walk." (Acts 3:6)

What is the point in all this? It has to do with our authority over sickness and disease. Authority doesn't ask or beg God to move on our behalf, authority speaks commands in faith. Jesus gave us authority over all manners of sickness and diseases, because we are seated with Him in heavenly places. Jesus wouldn't tell us to heal the sick if we had no authority to do so (Matthew 10:8).

"And these signs shall follow them that believe...they shall lay hands on the sick, and they shall recover."

(Mark 16:17-18)

"For the Son of man is as a man taking a far journey, who left his house, and gave authority to his servants, and to every man his work, and commanded the porter to watch." (Mark 13:34)

To beg God for something that has been provided to us in the Covenant we have with Christ, is a demonstration of unbelief in that Covenant blessing.

Since healing is indeed part of our Covenant with God, it changes the way in which we call for a healing. In order to please God, we must be in a place of faith, and faith believes the promises and provisions of the Covenant that we have through Christ. Begging for a healing is certainly not the prayer of faith we find in James 5:15. Notice that the only time we find the word prayer used for healing, we also discover that prayer for a healing is called a prayer of faith. "If it be God's will" is not a prayer of faith, but rather prayer of petition. He said to "Ask!" and you shall receive what you ask for when you believe! (Matthew 7:7; 21:22)

-KEY 7-

DEALING WITH
THE SPRIT

Occasionally people don't really need a healing, but they need deliverance. There are spirits of infirmity - Not all sickness is directly caused by demonic activity, but some certainly are. We each need spiritual discernment to know if it is a spiritual thing or a physical thing – Christians can become demon oppressed. Some people would say, "Well, a Christian can't have a demon." You can have whatever you want. So if you want to walk around with a spirit of infirmity, it's yours. So we can't get hooked up on if it's possessed, oppressed, depressed, unpressed, whatever it is. Go get rid of it. It's that simple, okay?

You know, some places, they get so stuck on, "Well, what do you mean, I have a spirit of infirmity?" I don't know. It's just what the Lord showed me. But do you want it? No! So let's get rid of it.

One of the most peculiar places I have ever had to deal with a spirit was in the pharmacy of a well-known shopping market. I call it the "Wal-Mart demon."

I wasn't looking for a deliverance session – I was there to buy cotton swabs. But as I was walking towards the pharmacy – I heard some commotion going on. Normally I would ignore such things, but sometimes you just know things are off and need your attention.

I stepped around the corner to find a young woman screaming at her mom. She was maybe 14-15 years old. For the sake of this story we will call her Amy. I walked up to the mom and I said, "Is everything okay?" She snidely responded in her southern accent, "Obviously not, I have never in my born days seen my daughter act like this."

The Lord immediately spoke to me "It's a spirit of yoga." (Note: I am not going to debate the idea of yoga being good or bad — I just listen and obey. If the Lord said it was a spirit of (insert whatever you want) I would deal with it.)

I said, "Ma'am (because that's what you say in the South), I am a pastor and I believe I can help." She looked at me like a deer in the headlights and kind of rolled her eyes, "Really? How?"

"Well, the Lord showed me that your daughter has a demon. Does she practice yoga?"

"Yes, my sister is a yogi and she is her apprentice."

"Okay, well I am going to cast the demon out."

She responded, "I'm Baptist, I don't believe in demons." (For all of my Baptist friends — I'm just relaying the story as it happened.)

By this time a small crowd was gathering. I turned to Amy and said, "Amy, I need to talk to you." As soon as I said that her face contorted and out of her gut came a deep raspy voice, "You can't have her, she's mine!"

I don't spend a lot of time dealing with demons so I simply responded, "You are a liar and I command you to shut up, you foul spirit."

I said again, "Amy I need to speak to you!" Her face normalized and I knew I was speaking to Amy. I said, "Amy, do you love Jesus?" "Yes, I do!" "Do you want this demon gone?" "Yes, I do!"

So I commanded the spirit to come out – it was not a tug of war. It was an exercise of my authority in Christ and the demon came out. I then got Amy filled with the Holy-Ghost (though her mom repeated she was Baptist and that she didn't believe in that either.)

While I do not believe God puts sickness on the believer because of a particular sin in their life. I do believe that we can get sick because we've opened doors which invite spirits that carry infirmities. While there are spirits of infirmity, many times other types of spirits carry infirmities with them, such as witchcraft, rebellion, the occult, anger, etc. People who get involved with witchcraft often wind up with physical infirmities that the witchcraft spirits have brought in with them. When doing deliverance on somebody, it is a good idea to bind the infirmities to the spirits as they are cast out.

Spirits, or demons, can come into one's life from a curse. A curse can afflict someone with sickness, poverty, addiction, constant failure, etc. It can also be generational. Curses, whether generational or from witchcraft, can be simply done away with by the blood of Jesus. It is simple, all you have to do is break the curse by the blood of Jesus and cancel its assignment. If the attack is still evident, continue to stand on the blood of Jesus, quote scripture, pray in tongues, and worship until it breaks. The Bible says, "Resist the Devil and he will flee from you." (James 4:7) Demons will always try and find their way back in through sin or agreement with the curse. "When you have done all to stand. Stand." (Ephesians 6:13). But do not, I repeat DO NOT, go on a demon hunt, it is a waste of your time, energy, and sanity. The Holy Spirit will show you if you are dealing with a spirit or a curse. And He will show you what to do, it's your job to be obedient

A curse can also be a legal right; a spirit carrying an infirmity is the means by which a curse is carried out. Matthew 18:21-35 shows where the tormenters do the tormenting, because they have a right to do it... a right given to them by sin in our hearts! In Matthew

18 the sin was unforgiveness. Unforgiveness is a legal right for spirits to indwell a person's body and inflict them with an infirmity.

Anytime a sickness is the result of a person's sin, it is not purely a physical healing that is needed, but rather a deliverance. A spirit carrying an infirmity has been let in, and needs to be driven out.

"Then a blind and dumb man under the power of a demon was brought to Jesus, and He cured him, so that the blind and dumb man both spoke and saw." (Matthew 12:22)

"And there was a woman there who for eighteen years had an infirmity caused by a spirit (a demon of sickness). She was bent completely forward and utterly unable to straighten herself up or to look upward. And when Jesus saw her, He called [her to Him] and said to her, Woman, you are released from your infirmity!" (Luke 13:11-12)

Many sicknesses are the result of a person being inflicted with a spirit carrying an infirmity, as we can see Jesus went about healing many who were oppressed of the devil:

"How God anointed Jesus of Nazareth with the Holy Ghost and with power: who went about doing good, and healing all that were oppressed of the devil; for God was with him." (Acts 10:38)

When dealing with somebody who has an infirmity, it's always a good idea to ask whether they have family members or ancestors who have had the same infirmity. It could be a generational spirit which has been going down the family line and needs to be cast out.

The ultimate goal however isn't to chase spirits or spend hours trying to figure out where a demon could've entered. We have much more authority than that. The ultimate goal is to "Listen" and then "obey!" If the Lord shows you there is a spirit, deal with it and move on.

-KEY 8-

OVERCOMING THE PAST

I opened the first chapter of the book with a story of a woman who had dealt with the disappointment of unanswered prayers. Past experiences have to be dealt with, however these experiences do not determine your future.

We all have had things in our past that have caused us disappointment even torment and pain, have made us question God's goodness or even if God could exist because of the things that happened. At the end of the day, your past only has power over you if you allow it to. You can stay in the torment, fear, pain, failure, defeat of the past or you can put to death the past and move forward in the newness of life Christ has given you.

I ministered to a woman I call the "Cherry pie lady." She stood in front of me as I ministered to her and I asked her what was going on. She said, "Well, 42 years ago I had a woman come over to my house and tell me she didn't care for my cherry pie and it has ruined my life."

Did you read that? *42 years!!!* She had allowed a woman's (who happened to be her mother) comments about her cherry pie to hold her in such bondage that it ruined her marriage, her ministry and everything else in her life. She did get free that day!

Other times when people have brought up their past (or current) trials they say to me, "What about Job?" Well, he's the example, not the rule. Let me remind you he lived before Jesus died. We're under a new Covenant. We're under the blood. So don't tell me, "Well, God afflicted Job." No, the enemy afflicted Job. Don't use him as an example. Get that out of your head. We have to look closely at what was really going on. Job saw God as a God who gave and took away, and later on in the book of Job, we find that God rebuked him for his way of thinking (Job 38:2) and Job repented for his foolish rants about the nature of God (Job 42:3). We like to quote Job's foolish rants as if they were scripture, and it just goes to show everybody how little we really understand the story of Job. That is wrongly dividing the Word of God and it has cost many people dearly because of the twisted picture of God which was fed to them from the pulpit. That's bad theology. Jesus died and finished the work. It's yours.

"You don't understand what I've been through..." You know, I'm sorry that you went through it. Jesus died and rose again. Your past does not determine your future. If you have received Jesus, your past was thrown in the garbage can. Stop digging it back up. We can't keep reliving our experiences. Move on. Are you going to let that experience keep you from your freedom here and now?

-Key 9-

Tenacity

You have got to be ferociously tenacious when it comes to contending for your miracle. "The Kingdom of heaven suffers violence and the violent take it by force!" I love how the amplified reads, "the Kingdom of heaven suffers violent assault, and violent men seize it by force [as a precious prize]." (Matt. 11:12)

Be stubborn.

In Matthew 15:21-28, we read of a mother who begged Jesus for help. Initially, He refuses her, yet she relentlessly continues pleading for her daughter's freedom.

"Leaving that place, Jesus withdrew to the region of Tyre and Sidon. A Canaanite woman from that vicinity came to him, crying out, "Lord, Son of David, have mercy on me! My daughter is suffering terribly from demon-possession."

Jesus did not answer a word. So his disciples came to him and urged him, "Send her away, for she keeps crying out after us." He answered, "I was sent only to the lost sheep of Israel." The woman came and knelt before him. "Lord, help me!" she said. He replied, "It is not right to take the children's bread and toss it to their dogs." "Yes, Lord," she said, "but even the dogs eat the crumbs that fall from their masters' table."

Then Jesus answered, "Woman, you have great faith! Your request is granted." And her daughter was healed from that very hour." (Matthew 15:21-28 NIV)

Her stubborn faith turned Christ's heart toward her and her child, granting what the woman requested.

Be relentless.

The parable of the persistent widow's story as accounted in Luke 18:1-5 illustrates how our determination can get us what we desire.

"One day Jesus told his disciples a story to show that they should always pray and never give up. [Did you see that Jesus wants to teach us how to pray and NEVER GIVE UP!] "There was a judge in a certain city," He said, "who neither feared God nor cared about people. A widow of that city came to him repeatedly, saying, 'Give me justice in this dispute with my enemy.' The judge ignored her for a while, but finally he said to himself, 'I don't fear God or care about people, but this woman is driving me crazy. I'm going to see that she gets justice, because she is wearing me out with her constant requests!'" (NLT)

Even as the authority (the judge) stood against her, she never let go of her hope. When Jesus comes back will you be found with this kind of relentless faith?

Be unshakable.

Samuel's mother Hannah probably couldn't have guessed that she'd bear a child, let alone one of the more influential prophets of the day. The despair she felt because of her physical barrenness could have crippled her faith. But, she continued to weep and pray for her miracle.

"And she made a vow, saying, 'O LORD Almighty, if you will only look upon your servant's misery and remember me, and not forget your servant but give her a son, then I will give him to the LORD for all the days of his life, and no razor shall ever touch his head.'

As she kept on praying to the LORD, Eli observed her mouth. Hannah was praying in her heart, and her lips were moving but her voice was not heard. Eli thought she was drunk and said to her, 'How long will you keep on getting drunk? Get rid of your wine.'

'Not so, my lord,' Hannah replied, "I am a woman who is deeply troubled. I have not been drinking wine or beer; I was pouring out my soul to the LORD. Do not take your servant for a wicked woman; I have been praying here out of my great anguish and grief."

Eli answered, "Go in peace, and may the God of

Israel grant you what you have asked of him." I Samuel 1:11-17 (NIV)

Hold onto your faith with such a tenacity that you are unshakable when it comes to following Him, relentless in seeking His guidance, and stubbornly persistent in asking for His mercy to fill your life.

-KEY 10-

OBEDIENCE

Obedience is probably one of the most important, if not the most important key to accessing the Kingdom. If you want the Kingdom of God to come in and invade your life, obey the word of the Lord. Jesus lived His life obeying the Father.

One way Jesus demonstrated a life of obedience was through His sensitivity to the Father's leading when there was someone before Him that was in need of healing. There was not one person healed the same way. We see many instances of Jesus healing blind eyes, yet there is not one story that is alike. For one man, He spit in his eyes (Mark 8:23); whereas, in another instance he spit on the dirt and made mud then had the man wash in the pool of Siloam (John 9:6-7). Still in another example, Jesus declared healing through spoken word, and the man's eyes opened (Luke 18:42).

I can recall many times that I saw the Kingdom manifested in my life because of obedience. One time, my wife and I were attending a conference at Joan Hunter's conference center, and the Lord spoke to me that we were to sow $1,000 into her ministry. Well, we didn't have $1,000 to give; in fact, we didn't have anything to give. The Lord told me, "I didn't ask you if you had $1,000." Therefore, we sowed a $1,000 on credit. That's right, credit! I couldn't believe it myself (not that I am condoning this; you MUST have a word from the Lord). What happened next blew us away. I can hardly summarize the numerous miracles of provision we saw released after this step of obedience.

Everywhere I went people bought my groceries. I would pull into a restaurant and they would give me my food for free. Pizza deliveries would come to my door, and the delivery   person would say that they had an order for Pastor Jacob and would give me a free pizza (exactly what I would have ordered in every instance). I would show up to the church, and bags of books and teachings would be waiting for me at the doorstep which, in and of itself, was a miracle considering the location of our church and the neighborhood surrounding it. I would walk into a store where a giveaway was taking place for a gift card, and I would win it! One person sowed tens of thousands of dollars into us which provided opportunities for personal needs to be met and for gifts and offerings to be shared with others.

Not only did I see miraculous provision released for me and my wife, but the first time I took my dog Charli with me to the church, I had brought an old pillow for her to lay on while I worked. Waiting for us at the door was a really nice dog mat and a $35 deer antler to keep her preoccupied. Did you catch that? Even my dog had favor!

All of what I shared above can be traced back to ONE simple step of obedience. I have had dreams where the Lord gave me specific directions, and when followed, tremendous blessing would come upon me. It has been my experience that obedience produces harvest. However, planting seeds of obedience does not always produce immediate harvest. A simple look at nature, proves this point. We don't always see the harvest after planting the seed. Nevertheless, harvest will come in due season if we are faithful to the task at hand.

Sometimes responding with obedience to the voice and leadership of the Lord can pose a great struggle for our flesh. However, the Lord honors obedience. When Namaan was told to wash seven times in the Jordan River by Elisha's servant, he got offended and was going to turn away. Thankfully, he had persistent servants who urged him saying, "My father, if the prophet had told you to do some great thing, would you not have done it? How much more then, when he has said to you, 'Wash, and be clean?'" (2 Kings 5:13 AMP). So in whatever God may ask you to do or to give, crucify your flesh (mind, will, and emotions) and be obedient. The Lord receives your offering of obedience and counts it to you as righteousness.

Obedience is what the Lord is asking for. There is no reward for those who live their lives repenting for disobedience. In 1 Samuel we find the phrase "obedience is better than sacrifice"; meaning it would be better to obey in the first place than have to repent for your disobedience. Just make the sacrifice and obey.

Deuteronomy 28:1-14 is a great passage of scripture that outlines the blessings of obedience.

"¹Now it shall be, if you diligently listen to and obey the voice of the Lord your God, being careful to do all of His commandments which I am commanding you today, the Lord your God will set you high above all the nations of the earth. [2]All these blessings will come upon you and overtake you if you pay attention to the voice of the Lord your God.

[3]"You will be blessed in the city, and you will be blessed in the field.

[4] "The [a]offspring of your [b]body and the produce of your ground and the offspring of your animals, the offspring of your herd and the young of your flock will be blessed.

[5] "Your basket and your kneading bowl will be blessed.

[6] "You will be blessed when you come in and you will be blessed when you go out.

[7] "The Lord will cause the enemies who rise up against you to be defeated before you; they will come out against you one way, but flee before you seven ways. [8] The Lord will command the blessing upon you in your storehouses and in [c]all that you undertake, and He will bless you in the land which the Lord your God gives you. [9] The Lord will establish you as a people holy [and set apart] to Himself, just as He has sworn to you, if you keep the commandments of the Lord your God and walk [that is, live your life each and every day] in His ways. [10] So

all the peoples of the earth will see that you are called by the name of the Lord, and they will be afraid of you. [11] The Lord will give you great prosperity, in the offspring of your body and in the offspring of your livestock and the produce of your ground, in the land which the Lord swore to your fathers to give you. [12] The Lord will open for you His good treasure house, the heavens, to give rain to your land in its season and to bless all the work of your hand; and you will lend to many nations, but you will not borrow. [13] The Lord will make you the head (leader) and not the tail (follower); and you will be above only, and you will not be beneath, if you listen and pay attention to the commandments of the Lord your God, which I am commanding you today, to observe them carefully. [14] Do not turn aside from any of the words which I am commanding you today, to the right or to the left, to follow and serve other gods.

So open your ears and hear what the Lord says (James 1:22). Then, DO IT! Whatever it may be, just be obedient to the voice and direction of the Lord.

-Final Key-

The Father is looking to bestow His goodness on you! Don't settle for anything less. It's my prayer for you to access the Kingdom that He is seeking to give to you. God not only wants us healed, Jesus has paid the price for our healing, and included it in His atoning work. That makes all the difference when it comes to God's will and how we minister healing.

Many times, physical infirmities are brought on by unclean spirits carrying infirmities, and in such cases we need to dig into the emotional and spiritual root of such cases. If it's there because of unforgiveness, then we need to get that person to forgive and then take them through emotional healing to clean up the emotional wound.

Once the emotional wound has been healed, we need to take authority over the sickness and the spirits which brought in the infirmity, and drive it out in Jesus' name.

It takes real faith to believe that we are totally forgiven of all our sins, and worthy to receive complete healing of our bodies because of the atonement of Christ which cost Jesus dearly. We need to change how we see God. We can't keep seeing Him through the eyes of religion, where God puts sickness on His people to teach them things. We need to start believing the Word of God straight up. Jesus made it very clear who came to kill, steal and destroy, versus who came that we might have life and have it more abundantly (John 10:10). If God's will for His people in the Old Covenant was that they all be healed and prosper, how much more would it be His will under the New Covenant, where healing and prosperity are actually a part of the atonement?

Just what if your miracle happened today? The possibilities are endless! The key is your hand, the door is in front of you – what will you do with what you have been given? Hear His invitation (or joy and laughter) as He waits for you to open the door. It's His good pleasure!

-KEYS TO VICTORY-

"IMPOSSIBILITY IS A LAUGHABLE WORD"

I heard the Lord clearly say "I laugh at the word impossibility." I was facing that word head on in some personal situations and I said "God, these are all impossible situations."

He replied -

"I laugh at the word impossibilities. Don't you see I've given you authority? The realm of impossibility belongs to you. I've given you that realm. For with man these things seem impossible, but with me impossibility doesn't even exist. I have not asked of you more than I expect you to deliver. I have equipped you with all of the necessary armor that you will need to go out in my name. I have equipped you and I will sustain you with My strength."

"Change your thinking. Change your world. Change your understanding of the word impossible and that through me - everything is possible. YOU are possible. Begin to declare, 'I'm possible! I'm possible" because of what I have done in you!

"I laugh at the word! I laugh at it. It's a laughable notion for you to use the word impossible. I laugh at the word impossibilities. I laugh! I urge you to begin to laugh at the word impossibilities. Laugh at it!"

"I've heard you say to me "God, this is impossible" and I just had to chuckle. I just had to laugh and say, "Oh you don't know me well enough yet. Don't you see - it's possible! Ha! Ha! It's so possible! Just begin to laugh at that word! Ha! Ha!"

"Don't you see, as you walk with me, impossibilities will leave your vocabulary. It's going to leave your thinking - you'll forget the word!"

"Impossible... Ha! Ha! Ha! All things are possible! You are my sons and daughters and I have given you the realm of impossibilities. I'm going to use you to make a laughingstock of the word - that wherever you go and whatever you do - whenever you are faced with that word you would laugh and see situations reversed. See those impossibilities become staggering awe-evoking miracles in the sight of those who would never believe."

"When you understand that when you live in me, you live in the realm of impossibility - when you live in me those things that were impossible are so easy! So laugh, laugh, laugh at the word because I am laughing right along with you," says the Lord.

Psalm 18:29 (paraphrased) - "With my God I can trample the hoard of hell, with my God I can jump over the word impossibilities."

SCRIPTURES TO STAND ON FOR HEALING

In the next few pages I have provided some scriptures for you to meditate on and pour over in the days to come as you contend for your healing.

Start by speaking these verses aloud. Meditate on them. Believe them. That's how we release God's power to heal—by speaking His Word and trusting His ability and His willingness to heal all of our diseases.

Psalm 103:1-3
BLESS (AFFECTIONATELY, gratefully praise) the Lord, O my soul; and all that is [deepest] within me, bless His holy name! Bless (affectionately, gratefully praise) the Lord, O my soul, and forget not [one of] all His benefits—

Who forgives [every one of] all your iniquities, Who heals [each one of] all your diseases.

Psalm 118:17
I shall not die but live, and shall declare the works and recount the illustrious acts of the Lord.

Psalm 147:3
He heals the brokenhearted and binds up their wounds [curing their pains and their sorrows].

Proverbs 4:20-22
My son, attend to my words; consent and submit to my sayings. Let them not depart from your sight; keep them in the center of your heart. For they are life to those who find them, healing and health to all their flesh.

Exodus 23:25
You shall serve the Lord your God; He shall bless your bread and water, and will take sickness from your midst.

Proverbs 3:7-8
Be not wise in your own eyes; reverently fear and worship the Lord and turn [entirely] away from evil. It shall be health to your nerves and sinews, and marrow and moistening to your bones.

Jeremiah 17:14
Heal me, O Lord, and I shall be healed; save me, and I shall be saved, for You are my praise.

Matthew 9:20-22

And behold, a woman who had suffered from a flow of blood for twelve years came up behind Him and touched the fringe of His garment; for she kept saying to herself, if I only touch His garment, I shall be restored to health. Jesus turned around and, seeing her, He said, Take courage, daughter! Your faith has made you well. And at once the woman was restored to health.

3 John 1:2

Beloved, I pray that you may prosper in every way and [that your body] may keep well, even as [I know] your soul keeps well and prospers.

Mark 16:17-18

And these attesting signs will accompany those who believe: in My name they will drive out demons; they will speak in new languages; they will pick up serpents; and [even] if they drink anything deadly, it will not hurt them; they will lay their hands on the sick, and they will get well.

Matthew 4:23-24

And He went about all Galilee, teaching in their synagogues and preaching the good news (Gospel) of the Kingdom, and healing every disease and every weakness and infirmity among the people. So the report of Him spread throughout all Syria, and they brought Him all who were sick, those afflicted with various diseases and torments, those under the power of demons, and epileptics, and paralyzed people, and He healed them.

Matthew 8:16-17
When evening came, they brought to Him many who were under the power of demons, and He drove out the spirits with a word and restored to health all who were sick. And thus He fulfilled what was spoken by the prophet Isaiah, He Himself took [in order to carry away] our weaknesses and infirmities and bore away our diseases.

James 5:14-15
Is anyone among you sick? He should call in the church elders (the spiritual guides). And they should pray over him, anointing him with oil in the Lord's name. And the prayer [that is] of faith will save him who is sick, and the Lord will restore him; and if he has committed sins, he will be forgiven.

Confession for physical healing:

"I know that it's God's will for me to be healthy and whole. I praise the Lord and thank Him for healing all of my diseases as I put my faith and trust in Him."

MEET THE AUTHOR

Jacob Biswell has the ability to clearly define the boundaries that the word of God has regarding living a life in the supernatural.

Having experienced many seasons of encounter with the Lord, he brings a much needed balance to the Body of Christ. Like few others, he can guide you through scripture to help you discern and discover your call to the destiny God has for you. His greatest heart's desire is to see Jesus and His bride get what He paid for.

As a prophetic voice, Jacob has served on multiple ministry boards providing apostolic insight. He is a highly sought after speaker both nationally and internationally. He speaks at conferences, churches and other events activating and empowering people to enter their destiny, grab hold of their dreams and receive their healing. Jacob flows with the Holy Spirit to wreak havoc on the Kingdom of Darkness and strengthen God's people.

Jacob is married to Anna Katheryn, daddy to Eden Grace and currently resides in Texas where they are the Lead Pastors of Living Word.

www.jacobbiswell.com

OTHER TITLES BY JACOB BISWELL

ENCOUNTERED

God wants to ENCOUNTER You!

"As I carefully opened my eyes, I was nearly blinded by the most radiant light have ever seen to this day... in all of his beauty, there he was. The person of Jesus. Love himself!"

Encountered takes you on one man's journey of visitations, open heavens and encounters which can only be described as supernatural.

Anyone can walk in the realm of encounter with the living God – even you!

Get ready to be encountered!

FOR ORDERING VISIT:

www.jacobbiswell.com

28037222R00050

Made in the USA
Columbia, SC
11 October 2018